GUERRILLAS OF GRACE

by Ted Loder

SAN DIEGO, CALIFORNIA

LuraMedia™

for Jan . . .
guerrilla of grace,
companion in faith,
gift of joy.

Other Books by Ted Loder
Tracks in the Straw (1985)
No One But Us (1986)
Eavesdropping on the Echoes (1987)
Wrestling the Light (1991)

International Standard Book Number 0-931055-04-0

Library of Congress Catalog Card Number 84-26096

Publisher's Catalog Number LM-601

Printed and Bound in the United States of America

LuraMedia
7060 Miramar Road, Suite 104
San Diego, California 92121

CONTENTS

Ground Me in Your Grace

Eternal One,
    Silence
        from whom my words come;
    Questioner
        from whom my questions arise;
    Lover
        of whom all my loves are hints;
    Disturber
        in whom alone I find my rest;
    Mystery
        in whose depths I find healing
            and myself;
enfold me now in your presence;
    restore to me your peace;
        renew me through your power;
           and ground me in your grace.

PROBING . . .

Why would anyone call a book of prayers, **GUERRILLAS OF GRACE**? The two images, "guerrillas" and "grace," seem to be an unlikely, if not contradictory, conjunction. And yet ... are they really?

Somewhere I read a description of poets as "guerrillas of beauty." I suppose it is fitting that I can't find the article, or even identify it, but the phrase struck me and took captive a piece of my imagination, as if demonstrating the power of the image. Or maybe it would be more accurate to say the phrase liberated a piece of my imagination. I began to see "guerrillas of beauty" as applying to the risky and exciting struggles of people attempting to live out their faith in more free and joyful ways in the midst of difficult, resistant, often even oppressive circumstances. I began to understand the phrase as applying well to people who pray and to the prayers they utter.

Yet, as important as I believe beauty is, and as powerful as I have experienced it to be, I think it is even more provocative to call those who pray, and the prayers themselves, "guerrillas of grace."

The notion of guerrillas seems to be rooted in the ancient Judeo-Christian tradition. The Old Testament prophets can easily be conceived of as guerrillas doing battle with the established powers of their day; and their thundering, poetic words and images surely can be read as forms of prayer. Certainly Jesus was the pre-eminent guerrilla of grace; he confronted repressive insti-tutions and liberated captive minds and hearts with his words and his life. A prime weapon in his effort was prayer, and it is little wonder that he taught his disciples to pray.

The early Christians understood and rallied to Paul's battle cry: "For we are not contending against flesh and blood, but against principalities, against powers, against the world rulers of this present darkness..." They, along with Christians across the ages, confirmed the idea that we are guerrillas.

There are two or three characteristics of guerrillas that give particular relevance to the use of that image to describe Christians. By any of our usual measures, guerrillas are a weaker force set against a superior and more organized power, a power which exerts both subtle and blatant pressures to conform. Such pressures are not commonly or quickly perceived or interpreted as oppressive, but frequently something in them is experienced as, at least, vaguely stifling to the spirit.

Guerrillas, then, are engaged in the battle to reclaim some territory, or some part of life, for a higher purpose, a truer cause. To wed guerrilla with grace suggests that the truer cause is God's kingdom. Since the "principalities and powers" are never completely "out there," but also stomp and rumble "within," a significant piece of the life to be reclaimed or liberated is the pray-er himself or herself. In an unavoidable way the struggle begins—and begins again and again and again—with choosing sides. Choose one side and you're a conformist; choose another and you're a guerrilla!

Doesn't "guerrilla" describe the contemporary church in China and Russia? Christians in those countries have been cut off from all typical religious support systems, yet have survived and grown in obviously hostile environments. Wasn't Dr. Martin Luther King, Jr.'s civil rights movement in the 1960's a non-violent guerrilla force, born and nurtured in the black church? Don't you suppose prayer was a critical part of what those Christians were about?

It is also important to note that guerrillas usually work in groups. In some fashion we never pray alone. We always pray toward someone and with someone—namely, whoever resides within us as teacher, friend, enemy, burden, brother, sister, spirit. However private our prayers may seem, we are still the cloud of witnesses when we pray (just as we are when we think or act). So, the prayers in this volume, though framed in personal terms, could easily be used as corporate prayers, and in many instances have been. The point is that both grace and guerrilla are relational terms.

And finally, guerrillas are never quite so desperate as they are confident. They believe they are fighting on the winning side, in spite of any and all appearances to the contrary. We have to be exceedingly careful in even considering this characteristic, for abuses perpetrated by religious arrogance are all too evident and painful. Still, guerrillas are willing to give their lives, if necessary, because they believe the cause for which they struggle, and which struggles in them, will finally prevail. Even so, the pray-er is always saying, one way or another, "... thy kingdom come."

Yet, prayer is always against the odds set by logic, by scientism, by realism. So, it is always against the odds of our own skepticism and doubt. Even when prayer is inchoate in something that sounds like a curse or a moan or a desperate plea or a spontaneous "whoopee," there is a gut deep, intuitive refusal to accept the odds or to calculate too closely either the limits of the possible or the sneakiness of grace.

When the prayer is more intentional, the guerrilla raid may at least suspend those odds for a bit longer and open the one who prays to broader dimensions of reality than he or she may have entertained before. Once that happens, there can never again be quite an end of it. Some part of us is taken captive or set free, and that shift changes the world a little. At those moments we also (and rightly) refuse to calculate what might be changed in the world beyond us , what might be gracefully released in it by our prayers.

It may be presumptuous to call oneself, and one's prayers, "guerrillas of grace." Grace is the sole property of God. It distinguishes the quality of God's love from human love. But then, how does grace become operative in the world? What is the process? Admittedly, those are large and complicated questions about which volumes have been and will be written, and which are beyond the scope of this introduction.

Still, one simple answer, and wondrous, is that God's grace operates in the world quite independently of us. Prayer is one way of attempting to focus on grace, to pay attention to it, to praise it. The French mystic Simone Weil is right in saying, "Perfect attention is prayer." Surely it is true that any attempts to be attentive, however imperfect, are also prayers. Imagination is crucial to paying attention, for attention is far more than observation. Imagination involves penetrating something, or being open to being penetrated by something, in order to sense its meaning, its possibilities, its depths, its "story."

Another simple answer, and equally wondrous, is that praying itself is part of the process by which grace becomes operative in the world. The pray-er becomes a participating point of the entry and expansion of grace, so that Augustine is also right in saying, "Without God, we cannot; without us, God will not."

In this sense imagination is crucial as a way of pre-figuring the shape or course the future may take. Imagination is an indispensable faculty in the process of deciding and acting toward the future. Thus, prayer can be playful because the imagination plays with possibilities, putting them together in different combinations before we begin to enact them. Since children are naturally adept at such play, perhaps that is one reason Jesus said, "Unless you turn and become

as children, you will never enter the kingdom of heaven." Since pre-figuring is an ongoing process, the imagination is always engaged in adjusting and reformulating. Thus, the future is always being partly created by the imagination of the pray-er and the prayer.

Therefore, since paying attention is one condition of prayer, the occasion of attending is a guerrilla action through which grace takes, or liberates, new ground in the praying person. Yet, through the mysterious dynamics of exchange, prayers and pray-ers themselves are the guerrilla action by which grace helps shape the future: "... without us, God will not." Prayer, through the process of imagination, becomes part of the answer to the remainder of the question, "Without us, God will not do what?" Prayer, as is faith or hope or love, is always guerrilla action in the world of time on behalf of the eternal.

Personally, my prayers happen in two ways. The first way, I believe, is nearly universal: the urgent, spontaneous outbursts, if not of half-formed words, fragmented and fleeting, then surely of a surge of emotions, sensations of awe or wonder or yearning which suddenly flood in and overflow to connect me, perhaps only in dim awareness, to the springs and rhythms of life and its impenetrable mysteries. I suppose only mystics and poets could, or should, even attempt to communicate these kinds of prayers with others, though these prayers are perhaps the most common. They are intensely personal and the type I most frequently mutter or moan.

The second way my prayers happen is as the more articulated works of my imagination. These are the kind of prayers contained in this book. Imagination is a basic faculty of faith and poetry, indeed, of any creative act. Imagination is surely one quality of God's image in us, just as is the capacity to love. For me, imagination is a way of gathering up the present and the immediate past—the things, persons, experiences to which I have been attentive, or sometimes just dully present—and putting them into images, into language which I hurl toward God and toward the future. Prayer is one way I participate in the ongoing creation. Prayer, through imagination, opens me and (I am presumptuous enough to contend) opens the future to new options, different possibilities. Imagination is a way of re-interpreting the past, re-viewing the present, and pre-viewing the future and the way I can act toward it. Imagination is a way of interrupting the programs for repetition into which I so easily set myself.

I have heard, with only partial understanding but with imagination, that the images of artists and poets often precede and instruct scientific discovery. If that is in any way true, the implications boggle the mind. Could it be that the images of poets and artists (and pray-ers) not only precede scientific discovery in some instances, but that they actually help create what the scientist later discovers? Indeed, could prayer be one of the fundamental ways "the universe becomes conscious of itself," to use that intriguing phrase by which some cosmologists explain not only how the universe seems to be unfolding, but why it is unfolding at all? But enough! I have strayed into depths well over my head.

Still, the depths themselves are an essential condition to acknowledge in prayer, at least for me. Depths swirl about the word "mystery," affirming that when we have to do with God, deep mystery is always one of the first conditions that pertain. God always outdistances our thoughts, words, knowledge, creeds, litanies, lives; outdistances them either because God is too simple for us to apprehend, or too complex for us to comprehend, or both.

An illustrative instance of what I am suggesting is the recent effort to de-sexualize the language and thinking of the church and to apply traditionally "feminine" characteristics to God. Such an effort is accurate and overdue! It opens us to dimensions of God we have missed and opens to God ways of being with us that have been denied. This experience of opening demonstrates what the richness of the depths of mystery means when referred to God, and how attentively exploring those depths liberates more territory for grace. That we explore those depths, and they us, makes us guerrillas of grace. But the unfathomable quality of mystery reminds us that it is the grace of God that we are exploring.

Mystery means that, in spite of all our efforts, all our insights, discoveries and experiences, we will never do much more than touch the hem of God's robe. It is enough that such touching brings healing. It is too much, idolatrously too much, to claim more than a very little information about the wearer of the robe. And even that little information, we can claim only with enormous humility. However, humility is the twin of trust.

It has been said, referring to the temptation to which biblical literalists often succumb, that we should never confuse the love letter with the lover. We all have our version of such literalism, our dogmaticisms, our exaggerated (if unadmitted) claims of knowledge. Humble acknowledgement of mystery delivers us from the imprisonment of such certainties into the awesome dimensions of possibilities. Trust begins there. So, in some primitive way, does prayer.

Historically, the church has used the term "holy" to refer to what I mean by the word "mystery." My bias for the word mystery is grounded in the awareness that holiness is a term which often has been too well defined and too aggressively applied in too many inquisitions. Jesus gave the mystery a personal name, as did the prophets, but Jesus did not thereby eliminate or domesticate the mystery. The point is, mystery simply reminds us that God is free to be God in ways we have no knowledge of at all.

Since God is free to respond to prayers in surprising, sneaky ways (you may have noticed I like the word "sneaky") that no one can prescribe, we also are free to do new things, pray new ways, imagine new images, find different words. We are never required to be liturgical literalists. We are never restricted merely to repeating the prayers of our tradition, however beautiful and helpful. Nor are there "right" prayers, or "right" ways of praying, or "right" words with which to pray. Guerrillas extend grace, not encapsulate it.

So, the second way I pray, articulating from my imagination, involves work! There are people who insist that the only prayers which are valid are those offered spontaneously at the immediate inspiration of the Holy Spirit. Such prayers certainly are valid, but they are also usually more inchoate than inspired or inspiring, and they tend to be repetitious and dull. I believe the Holy Spirit inspires me just as well when I am struggling to think, to attend, to write, to find the appropriate words, symbols, images which will open me, and perhaps those who pray with me, to those new perceptions and possibilities that hint of grace.

Poet John Ciardi states that the poets' morality resides in "never cheapening their choices" of words or images. I concur and think it is almost immoral for a person consistently to cheapen his or her prayer choices by trying to avoid the cost of paying attention, for attention does have a cost. I think it is almost immoral, and certainly lazy, for anyone not to work carefully and honestly to shape prayers since, "...without us, God will not." And probably "God will not" without our best efforts! Who dares to be a sloppy guerrilla? Who deserves one?

So, my attempts to pray, to use my imagination as I pray, involve three factors. The first is to express–through words, images, symbols–what I see, feel, attend to and experience, but to do so in ways that both sharpen my awareness and perhaps provide me and my companion guerrillas a shift in perception, a slightly different way of seeing, interpreting and responding to life. In that shift, however slight, I believe my prayers are already being answered. The guerrilla process has begun because the shift involves probing, reaching, playing with different images and options which are changing me. Grace is sneaky!

The second aspect of imaginative praying is to be open to words, thoughts, feelings, visions and alternatives which bubble up or float down when I am struggling to find a way to be honest and creative and to have some integrity in that prayer process. Sometimes the muse does ride, or better, the Spirit does move. But often the impulse or image that comes seems, at first blush, to be too radical or profane or outrageous to be acceptable or to use. But that may be exactly the time to work at staying open and following the lead, the intuition, the inspiration. Passion, which is surely part of praying just as centering and quietness are, is not always nice or proper! Unfortunately, passion seldom seems to be part of what we have been taught is involved in being religious or praying. Passion touches on one reason I like the prayer included

in this volume which adds to the familiar phrase describing God as being the one "from whom no secrets are hid" another phrase: "and none need to be."* Grace is sneaky, not superficial.

The third factor in my praying is to let my prayer carry me. I saw an expression somewhere which asked, "If you aren't carried away, why go?" There is at least some delightful truth in that, except that the rest also needs saying: namely, for the most part, you don't get carried away if you don't hoist your sails to the wind by doing the work of preparation and persistence.

But often, because of our anxieties about control and losing it, when the wind starts to blow we tend to lower our sails. Once new possibilities start to emerge, once the future gets imaged differently, once the impulse tugs to try an option other than the familiar rut, then the inner and outer argument begins. The limits of what is possible start to get calculated "realistically" again. The ballast of odds becomes heavy. The territory which had begun to be freed by the guerrillas of grace gets retaken by the armies of conformity and caution. Is this true for you, too, or do I refer only to myself?

It has taken me a long time and hard struggle even to begin to wrestle effectively with this third factor. Mostly it still pins me without giving me a blessing. I've discovered that it has something to do with expectations. On the one hand, we can expect too much, too fast, and give up praying when it doesn't happen. Jesus, and saints since, have said much

12

* "I Am So Thankful to Be Alive," page 40.

about this danger. Yet, on the other hand, we can get frightened and give up praying when different options do emerge and we are nudged toward them. However much we talk about our longing for change in ourselves and the world, the actual prospect of that change, and the cost of it in terms of engaging in battle with the powers of conformity, produces some ambivalence at best. Ambivalence generates resistance. It is hard to get carried away when we're hanging on tightly to the familiar.

I'm discovering that getting carried away doesn't necessarily mean moving at the speed of light or to the gates of heaven (or whatever you envision as a quick escape, or a safe haven from the toil and trouble of change). It may mean being carried away as a stoker on a slow freighter, as it were. For me, the process of being carried away does happen slowly, even painfully, albeit joyfully, an inch a day, another at night, for a lifetime. But I am getting there. Grace is sneaky and persistent!

Being carried away also involves, for me, some intentional participation in the mystery, some attempt to embody the images and exhibit the perceptions of some piece of my prayers. It involves willingly, perhaps foolishly, taking the risk about which we are warned in the old joke, "Be careful what you pray for; you may get it." But, isn't that possibility precisely why pray-ers are guerrillas of grace?

So you see, I cannot believe that praying doesn't make a difference. If it doesn't, what else could?

For at last I believe
    life itself is a prayer,
and the prayers we say
    shape the lives we live,
just as the lives we live
    shape the prayers we say;
and it all shapes the kingdom
    which expresses itself in and among us,
      and for which we are guerrillas.
I hope these prayers help you
    to take some new territory,
      to liberate imaginatively some part of your life,
    my sister and brother guerrillas.
      "... thy kingdom come ..."

- Ted Loder

Prayers of
Quietness & Listening

Listen to Me Under My Words

O God,
I come to you now
as a child to my Mother,
    out of the cold which numbs
        into the warm who cares.
Listen to me inside,
    under my words
        where the shivering is,
    in the fears
        which freeze my living,
    in the angers
        which chafe my attending,
    in the doubts
        which chill my hoping,
    in the events
        which shrivel my thanking,
    in the pretenses
        which stiffen my loving.

Listen to me, Lord,
as a Mother,
    and hold me warm,
        and forgive me.
Soften my experiences
    into wisdom,
my pride
    into acceptance,
my longing
    into trust,
and soften me
    into love
        and to others
           and to you.

Guide Me into an Unclenched Moment

Gentle me,
Holy One,
into an unclenched moment,
    a deep breath,
        a letting go
            of heavy expectancies,
                of shriveling anxieties,
                    of dead certainties,
that, softened by the silence,
    surrounded by the light,
        and open to the mystery,
I may be found by wholeness,
    upheld by the unfathomable,
        entranced by the simple,
            and filled with the joy
                that is you.

Hear Me Quickly, Lord

Hear me quickly, Lord
for my mind soon wanders to other things
  I am more familiar with
    and more concerned about
      than I am with you.
O Timeless God, for whom I do not have time,
catch me with a sudden stab of beauty
  or pain
    or regret
that will catch me up short for a moment
to look hard enough at myself —
  the unutterable terror
    and hope within me —
and, so, to be caught by you.

Words will not do, Lord.
Listen to my tears,
  for I have lost much
    and fear more.
Listen to my sweat,
  for I wake at night
    overwhelmed by darkness and strange dreams.
Listen to my sighs,
  for my longing surges like the sea —
    urgent, mysterious and beckoning.
Listen to my heart beat,
  for I want to live fully
    and stay death forever.
Listen to my breathing,
  for I gulp after something like holiness.
Listen to my clenched teeth,
  for I gnaw at my grudges
    and forgive myself as reluctantly
      as I forgive others.

Listen to my growling gut,
    for I hunger for bread and intimacy.
Listen to my curses,
    for I am angry at the way the world
        comes down on me sometimes,
        and I sometimes on it.
Listen to my cracking knuckles,
    for I hold very tightly to myself
        and anxiously squeeze myself
            into other's expectations,
                and them into mine,
      and then shake my fists at you
        for disappointing me.
Listen to my sex,
    for I seek fulfillment
        through the man-woman differences
        and beyond the differences,
           a new, common humanity.
Listen to my foot falls,
    for I stumble to bring good tidings to someone.
Listen to my groans,
    for I ache toward healing.
Listen to my worried weariness,
    for my work matters much to me
        and needs help.
Listen to my tension,
    for I stretch toward accepting who I am
        and who I cannot be.
Listen to my wrinkles,
    for growing years make each day
        singularly precious to me
           and bring eternity breathtakingly close.

Listen to my hunched back,
        for sometimes I can't bear
                the needs and demands of the world anymore
                    and want to put it down,
                        give it back to you.
Listen to my laughter,
        for there are friends
            and mercy
                and the day grows longer,
                    and something urges me to thank.
Listen to my humming,
        for sometimes I catch all unaware
            the rhythms of creation
        and then music without words
            rises in me to meet it,
                and there is the joy of romping children
                    and dancing angels.
Listen to my blinking eyes,
        for at certain moments
            when sunlight strikes just right,
            or stars pierce the darkness just enough,
            or clouds roll around just so,
            or snow kisses the earth into quietness,
        everything is suddenly transparent,
            and crows announce the presence of another world,
            and dogs bark at it,
        and something in me is pure enough
            for an instant
        to see your kingdom in a glance,
        and so to praise you in a gasp —
            quick,
                then gone,
                    but it is enough.

Listen to me quickly, Lord.

Calm Me into a Quietness

Now,
O Lord,
calm me into a quietness
    that heals
        and listens,
and molds my longings
    and passions,
        my wounds
            and wonderings
into a more holy
    and human
        shape.

I Need to Breathe Deeply

Eternal Friend,
grant me an ease
to breathe deeply of this moment,
        this light,
                this miracle of now.
Beneath the din and fury
        of great movements
                and harsh news
                        and urgent crises,
make me attentive still
        to good news,
                to small occasions,
                        and the grace of what is possible
                                for me to be,
                                        to do,
                                                to give,
                                                        to receive,
that I may miss neither my neighbor's gift
        nor my enemy's need.

Precious Lord,
grant me
    a sense of humor
        that adds perspective to compassion,
    gratitude
        that adds persistence to courage,
    quietness of spirit
        that adds irrepressibility to hope,
    openness of mind
        that adds surprise to joy;
that with gladness of heart
I may link arm and aim
with the One who saw signs of your kingdom
    in salt and yeast,
        pearls and seeds,
            travelers and tax collectors,
                sowers and harlots,
                    foreigners and fishermen,
and who opens my eyes with these signs
    and my ears with the summons
        to follow to something more
            of justice and joy.

In the Silence, Name Me

Holy One,
    untamed
        by the names
            I give you,
in the silence
    name me,
that I may know
    who I am,
hear the truth
    you have put into me,
trust the love
    you have for me,
        which you call me to live out
            with my sisters and brothers
                in your human family.

Help Me Listen

O Holy One,
I hear and say so many words,
yet yours is the word I need.
Speak now,
and help me listen;
and, if what I hear is silence,
    let it quiet me,
      let it disturb me,
        let it touch my need,
          let it break my pride,
            let it shrink my certainties,
              let it enlarge my wonder.

It Would Be Easier to Pray if I Were Clear

O Eternal One,
it would be easier for me to pray
    if I were clear
        and of a single mind and a pure heart;
    if I could be done hiding from myself
        and from you, even in my prayers.
But, I am who I am,
    mixture of motives and excuses,
        blur of memories,
            quiver of hopes,
    knot of fear,
        tangle of confusion,
            and restless with love,
                for love.
I wander somewhere between
    gratitude and grievance,
        wonder and routine,
            high resolve and undone dreams,
                generous impulses and unpaid bills.
Come, find me, Lord.
Be with me exactly as I am.
Help me find me, Lord.
    Help me accept what I am,
        so I can begin to be yours.
Make of me something small enough to snuggle,
    young enough to question,
        simple enough to giggle,
            old enough to forget,
                foolish enough to act for peace;
    skeptical enough to doubt
        the sufficiency of anything but you,
    and attentive enough to listen
        as you call me out of the tomb of my timidity
            into the chancy glory of my possibilities
                and the power of your presence.

Grant Me an Enchantment of Heart

O God of children and clowns,
    as well as martyrs and bishops,
somehow you always seem to tumble
    a jester or two of light
        through the cracks of my proud defense
           into the shadows of my sober piety.
Grant me, now, an enchantment of heart
that, for a moment,
the calliope of your kingdom
may entice my spirit,
    laughing,
out of my sulky self-preoccupations
into a childlike delight
    in the sounds and silences
        that hum of grace;
so I may learn again
that life is never quite as serious as I suppose,
yet more precious than I dare take for granted,
    even for a moment;
that I may be released
    into the possibilities of the immediate,
and rush,
    smudge souled as I am,
        to join the parade of undamned fools
           who see the ridiculous in the sublime,
           the sublime in the ridiculous;
and so dare to take pratfalls for love,
    walk tightropes for justice,
        tame lions for peace,
and rejoice to travel light,
    knowing there is little I have or need
        except my brothers and sisters to love,
           you to trust,
             and your stars to follow home.

Lead Me Out of My Doubts and Fears

Eternal God,
lead me now
    out of the familiar setting
        of my doubts and fears,
    beyond my pride
        and my need to be secure
into a strange and graceful ease
    with my true proportions
        and with yours;
that in boundless silence
    I may grow
        strong enough to endure
            and flexible enough to share
                your grace.

Give Me Ears to Hear

Lord,
I believe
    my life is touched by you,
        that you want something for me,
           and of me.
Give me ears
    to hear you,
eyes
    to see the tracing of your finger,
and a heart
    quickened by the motions
        of your Spirit.

Prayers of
Thanks & Praise

Praise from All Creatures, Laughers, and List-Makers

Praise be to you, O Lord,
who spins shining stars across the wondrous heavens
    and stretches out the seas,
who lifts the dawn into place
    and sets boundaries for night,
who awes the earth with storms
    and gentles it with green,
who gives everything a season
    and breathes life and love into the dust of me.
Praise be to you.

Praise in all things,
    for all things:
the soft slant of sunlight,
    the sweat of battle,
a song in the wilderness,
    the evening breeze,
the deep breath,
    the tended wound,
mercy, quietness, a friend;
for the miracles of the daily,
    the mysteries of the eternal.
Praise be to you.

Praise from all creatures,
    laughers and list-makers,
        wonders and worriers,
            poets and plodders and prophets,
          the wrinkled, the newborn,
            the whale, and the worm,
          from all,
            and from me.
Praise,
praise be to you
for amazing grace.

Bless What Eludes My Grasp

Lord, so many things skitter through my mind,
and I give chase to gather them
 and hold them up in a bunch to you,
but they go this way and that
 while I go that way and this ...
So, gather me up instead
and bless what eludes my grasp but not yours:
 trees and bees,
 fireflies and butterflies,
 roses and barbeques,
 and people ...
Lord, the people ... bless the people:
 birthday people,
 giving birth people,
 being born people;
 conformed people,
 dying people,
 dead people;
 hostaged people,
 banged up people,
 held down people;
 leader people,
 lonely people,
 limping people;
 hungry people,
 surfeited people,
 indifferent people;
 first world people,
 second world people,
 third world people;
 one world people,
 your people,
 all people.
Bless them, Lord.
Bless what eludes my grasp but not yours.

Praise Be to You for Life

Praise be to you, O Lord, for life
    and for my intense desire to live;
praise be to you for the mystery of love
    and for my intense desire to be a lover;
praise be to you for this day
    and another chance to live and love.

Thank you, Lord,
    for friends who stake their claim in my heart,
    for enemies who disturb my soul and bump my ego,
    for tuba players,
        and story tellers,
           and trapeze troupes.
Thank you, Lord,
    for singers of songs,
    for teachers of songs,
        who help me sing along the way,
    . . . and for listeners.
Thank you, Lord,
    for those who attempt beauty
        rather than curse ugliness,
    for those who take stands
        rather than take polls,
    for those who risk being right
        rather than pandering to be liked,
    for those who do something
        rather than talking about everything.

Lord, grant me grace, then,
and a portion of your spirit
that I may so live
    as to give others cause
        to be thankful for me,
thankful because I have not forgotten
    how to hope,
        how to laugh,
            how to say, "I'm sorry,"
    how to forgive,
        how to bind up wounds,
            how to dream,
    how to cry,
        how to pray,
    how to love when it is hard,
        and how to dare when it is dangerous.
Undamn me, Lord,
that praise may flow more easily from me
    than wants,
thanks more readily
    than complaints.
Praise be to you, Lord, for life;
praise be to you for another chance to live.

I Praise You for What Is Yet to Be

Wondrous Worker of Wonders,
I praise you
not alone for what has been,
    or for what is,
        but for what is yet to be,
for you are gracious beyond all telling of it.

I praise you
that out of the turbulence of my life
    a kingdom is coming,
        is being shaped even now
            out of my slivers of loving,
                my bits of trusting,
                my sprigs of hoping,
                my tootles of laughing,
                my drips of crying,
                my smidgens of worshipping;
that out of my songs and struggles,
    out of my griefs and triumphs,
        I am gathered up and saved,
for you are gracious beyond all telling of it.

I praise you
that you turn me loose
    to go with you to the edge of now and maybe,
        to welcome the new,
            to see my possibilities,
                to accept my limits,
and yet begin living to the limit
    of passion and compassion
        until,
            released by joy,
I uncurl to other people
    and to your kingdom coming,
for you are gracious beyond all telling of it.

Thank You for Each Moment

Lord, thank you for each moment,
    for the blue-sky moment,
        the softening earth,
            the freshening wind,
    for the sap flowing,
        the bird nesting,
            the yellow bush,
    for my full heart
        and the joy rising in me.
Soften me
    to receive whatever comes as a gift
        and to praise you in it.

Lord, thank you for each moment,
    for the twilight moment,
        the pause,
            the good tired,
    for the quiet reflection,
        the slowing down,
            the mysterious sunset,
    for my contented heart
        and the wisdom growing inside me.
Gentle me
    to feel whatever comes as a gift
        and to praise you in it.

Lord, thank you for each moment,
    for the midnight moment,
        the loneliness,
            the fretful wondering,
    for the watchful stars,
        the long ache,
            the sleepless wait,
    for my restless heart
        and the hope straining in me.

Focus me
    to see whatever comes as a gift
        and to praise you in it.

Lord, thank you for each moment,
    for the high-noon moment,
        the job,
            the necessary routine,
    for the sweaty struggle,
        the high risk challenge,
            the impulse to change,
    for my fierce heart
        and the courage gathering in me.
Ground me
    to wrestle with whatever comes as a gift
        and to praise you in it.

Lord, thank you for each moment,
    for the shared moment,
        the listening,
            the unguarded word,
    for the fragile openness,
        the ready smile,
            the accepted difference,
    for my passionate heart
        and the trust rooting in me.
Stretch me
    to grow with whatever comes as a gift
        and to praise you in it.

Lord, thank you for each moment,
    for the charged moment,
        the confrontation,
            the accurate demand,
    for the hard decision,
        the breathless gamble,
            the unexpected growing,
    for my intense heart
        and the truth expanding in me.
Excite me
    to be open to whatever comes as a gift
        and to praise you in it.

Lord, thank you for each moment,
    for the holy moment,
        the music,
            the child's eyes,
    for the sunlight,
        the touch,
            the tears,
    for the trembling pleasure,
        the unutterable beauty,
            the breathing,
    for the life and love and heart in me, aware,
        and the wholeness spreading in me.
Touch me
    through whatever comes as a gift
        that I may be graceful
            and praise you in it all.

I Am So Thankful to Be Alive

Persistent Friend,
    Insistent Enemy,
        from whom no secret is hid
        (and none need to be),
out of the thoughts and feelings which whirl within,
I grope for language to carry to you
    my secrets and all the wonders
        that seize my heart.
Praise be to you
    for holding me in the womb of mystery
        through all the eons of creation until now
    and raising me to life
        in this time and place.
I am so thankful to be alive —
    breathing, moving, sensing,
        wide-eyed, cock-eared alive —
in this mysterious instant,
    at this luminous time,
        on this nurturing earth,
            this blue pearl of great price
                whirling through uncharted space,
                attended by vigilant stars;
during these days of chance and battle,
    with streaks of hope and holiness on the horizon,
        touched by nature's pleading beauty
        and friendship's steady hold.
I am so thankful to be alive —
    eyes in love with seeing,
        ears in love with hearing,
            heart in love with attending,
                mind in love with connecting;
eager to miss no message of grace
    in the ballet of beauty
        or in the cramp of struggle
            of this incredible gift of life;

attentive to all the clues of love,
    daringly and outlandishly
        scattered for me through Jesus' life,
           overturning habit and hate;
attentive to the dreams he renews,
    the wounds he heals,
        the promises he nails up
           for me to step out on.
I am so thankful to be alive,
thankful for those times
    when the rhythms of my life
        catch the cadences of your kingdom,
    when there is a lightening in me
        for a moment,
    when the creep of courage
        allows me to dare to serve the gifts
           you have put in me;
thankful for the neighbors you have put beside me,
    and the possibilities you have put before me;
thankful for the surge of determination
    to accept difficulty
        not as an excuse for passivity,
          but as a goad to creativity,
            as the door to abundant life,
             and the seed of a peace
              the world cannot take away,
               as it takes away so much else.
I am so thankful to be alive,
    O Persistent Friend,
        Insistent Enemy;
hold me always in the womb of mystery
    and raise me again
        and again,
           forever,
to life,
    and to love,
        and to the claims of your kingdom.

I Thank You for Those Things that Are Yet Possible

O God of timelessness
     and time,
I thank you for my time
and for those things that are yet possible
     and precious in it:
          daybreak and beginning again,
               midnight and the touch of angels,
                    the taming of demons in the dance of dreams;
a word of forgiveness,
     and sometimes a song,
for my breathing . . . my life.

Thank you
for the honesty which marks friends
     and makes laughter;
for fierce gentleness
     which dares to speak the truth in love
          and tugs me to join the long march toward peace;
for the sudden gusts of grace
     which rise unexpectedly in my wending from dawn to dawn;
for children unabashed,
     wind rippling a rain puddle,
          a mockingbird in the darkness,
               a colleague and a cup of coffee;
for all the mysteries of loving,
     of my body next to another's body;
for music and silence,
     for wrens and Orion,
          for everything that moves me to tears,
               to touching,
                    to dreams,
                         to prayers;
for my longing . . . my life.

Thank you
for work
     which engages me in an internal debate
         between right and reward
    and stretches me toward responsibility
        to those who pay for my work,
           and to those who cannot pay
              because they have no work;
for justice
    which repairs the devastations of poverty;
for liberty
    which extends to the captives of violence;
for healing
    which binds up the broken bodied
      and broken hearted;
for bread broken
    for all the hungry of the earth;
for good news
    of love which is stronger than death;
and for peace
    for all to sit under fig trees
      and not be afraid;
for my calling . . . my life.

Thank you
for the sharp senses
    of the timeless stirring in my time,
      and your praise in my heart;
for the undeniable awareness, quick as now,
    that the need of you
      is the truth of me,
    and your presence with me
      is the truth of you,
    which sets me free
      for others,
        for joy,
          and for you;
for your grace . . . my life . . . forever.

Prayers of
Unburdening & Confession

Empty Me

Gracious and Holy One,
    creator of all things
        and of emptiness,
I come to you
    full of much that clutters and distracts,
        stifles and burdens me,
            and makes me a burden to others.
Empty me now
    of gnawing dissatisfactions,
        of anxious imaginings,
            of fretful preoccupations,
    of nagging prejudices,
        of old scores to settle,
            and of the arrogance of being right.
Empty me
    of the ways I unthinkingly
        think of myself as powerless,
            as a victim,
    as determined by sex, age, race,
        as being less than I am,
            or as other than yours.
Empty me
    of the disguises and lies
        in which I hide myself
            from other people
    and from my responsibility
        for my neighbors
            and for the world.
Hollow out in me a space
    in which I will find myself,
find peace and a whole heart,
    a forgiving spirit and holiness,
        the springs of laughter,
and the will to reach boldly
    for abundant life for myself
        and the whole human family.

Drive Me Deep to Face Myself

Lord, grant me your peace,
    for I have made peace
        with what does not give peace,
and I am afraid.
Drive me deep, now,
    to face myself so I may see
that what I truly need to fear is
    my capacity to deceive
        and willingness to be deceived,
    my loving of things
        and using of people,
    my struggle for power
        and shrinking of soul,
    my addiction to comfort
        and sedation of conscience,
    my readiness to criticize
        and reluctance to create,
    my clamor for privilege
        and silence at injustice,
    my seeking for security
        and forsaking the kingdom.

Lord, grant me your peace.
Instill in me such fear of you
    as will begin to make me wise,
and such quiet courage
    as will enable me to begin
        to make hope visible,
            forgiving delightful,
                loving contagious,
                    faith liberating,
                        peace-making joyful
and myself open
    and present
        to other people
            and your kingdom.

Loosen My Grip

O God, it is hard for me to let go,
    most times,
and the squeeze I exert
    garbles me and gnarls others.
So, loosen my grip a bit
    on the good times,
        on the moments of sunlight and star shine and joy,
that the thousand graces they scatter as they pass
    may nurture growth in me
        rather than turn to brittle memories.

Loosen my grip
    on those grudges and grievances
        I hold so closely,
that I may risk exposing myself
    to the spirit of forgiving and forgiveness
        that changes things and resurrects dreams and courage.

Loosen my grip
    on my fears
that I may be released a little into humility
    and into an acceptance of my humanity.

Loosen my grip
    on myself
that I may experience the freedom of a fool
    who knows that to believe
            is to see kingdoms, find power, sense glory;
    to reach out
            is to know myself held;
    to laugh at myself
            is to be in on the joke of your grace;
    to attend to each moment
            is to hear the faint melody of eternity;
    to dare love
            is to smell the wild flowers of heaven.

Loosen my grip
    on my ways and words,
            on my fears and fretfulness
that letting go
    into the depths of silence
            and my own uncharted longings,
I may find myself held by you
    and linked anew to all life
            in this wild and wondrous world
                    you love so much,
so I may take to heart
    that you have taken me to heart.

Release Me

O Holy and Haunting Presence
whose spirit moves quietly
    but surely
in the sound and fury of the world
    and of my life,
you know me
    as rushing water knows the rock
        and releases its beauty
            to reflect new light.
Open me
    to the insistent abrasiveness of your grace,
        for I often trivialize love
            by abandoning the struggles
                which accompany its joys
            and rejecting the changes
                which lead to its fulfillments.
Release me
    from the dark fury
        of assuming I am unloved
    when the day calls for sacrifice
        and the night for courage.

Release me
from the ominous fear
of thinking some sin
or failure of mine
can separate me from you
when life demands hard choices,
and the battle, high risks.
Release me
from the dangerous illusions
of independence
when the human family summons me
to the realities and promises
of interdependence
among races, sexes, nations.
Release me
from being possessed
by riches I do not need
and grievances that weary me
when you call me to share
my very self
with neighbors
and to reflect for the world
the light of the kingdom
within me.

What Can I Believe?

O God, I am so fragile:
    my dreams get broken,
    my relationships get broken,
    my heart gets broken,
    my body gets broken.

What can I believe,
    except that you will not despise a broken heart,
    that old and broken people shall yet dream dreams,
    and that the lame shall leap for joy,
        the blind see,
            the deaf hear.

What can I believe,
    except what Jesus taught:
    that only what is first broken, like bread,
        can be shared;
    that only what is broken
        is open to your entry;
    that old wineskins must be ripped open and replaced
        if the wine of new life is to expand.

So, I believe, Lord;
help my unbelief
    that I may have courage to keep trying
        when I am tired,
    and to keep wanting passionately
        when I am found wanting.

O God, I am so frail:
    my life spins like a top,
        bounced about by the clumsy hands
            of demands beyond my doing,
    fanned by furies
        at a pace but half a step from hysteria,
          so much to do,
             my days so few and fast-spent,
               and I mostly unable to recall
                  what I am rushing after.

What can I believe,
    except that beyond the limits
        of my little prayers and careful creeds,
    I am not meant for dust and darkness,
        but for dancing life and silver starlight.

Help my unbelief
    that I may have courage
        to dare to love the enemies
           I have the integrity to make;
        to care for little else
           save my brothers and sisters of the human family;
        to take time to be truly with them,
           take time to see,
             take time to speak,
               take time to learn with them
                  before time takes us;
        and to fear failure and death less
           than the faithlessness
              of not embracing love's risks.

God, I am so frantic:
    somehow I've lost my gentleness
        in a flood of ambition,
    lost my sense of wonder
        in a maze of videos and computers,
    lost my integrity
        in a shuffle of commercial disguises,
    lost my gratitude
        in a swarm of criticisms and complaints,
    lost my innocence
        in a sea of betrayals and compromises.

What can I believe,
    except that the touch of your mercy
        will ease the anguish of my memory;
    that the tug of your spirit
        will empower me to help carry now the burdens
            I have loaded on the lives of others;
    that the example of Jesus
        will inspire me to find again my humanity.

So, I believe, Lord;
help my unbelief
    that I may have courage
        to cut free from what I have been
    and gamble on what I can be,
        and on what you
            might laughingly do
                with trembling me
                    for your incredible world.

Unlock the Door of My Heart

Jesus said,
    "Your sins are forgiven;
        rise and walk."
Forgiveness is an unlocked door
    to walk through
        into a wide-whoopee-open world.
Forgiveness is a seed
    to water with new dreams and wild risks
        until it bears unexpected fruit.
Forgiveness is an enemy-friend
    to be born out of,
        a quietness beneath the clamor.
Forgiveness is a flower to smell,
    a wind at my back,
        a gull to scream with,
    a pain to laugh beneath,
        a burden that carries me.
It is I
    becoming We
        becoming Yours.
Forgiveness is a song to sing.
    O Lord,
        unlock the door of my heart.

I Care

Holy One,
most of the time you don't seem very close
    or real to me —
only a word,
    an ought,
        a longing, maybe,
            a hope —
and, for the most part,
I don't care much about you,
and that is the not-so-pretty truth of it.

But there are things I do care about:
    myself mostly,
        and some people I feel close to —
            families, friends, children,
                most of all children.
I do care what happens to them.

So, I do care about love,
    about being loved,
        and about loving
            (or trying to);
and I wonder about it,
    how to do it,
        and what makes me want to do it.

With those close to me,
    I care about laughing,
        and crying,
        and learning,
            and talking honestly (a little);
    and fighting openly and fairly,
        and forgiving (a bit more),
            and admitting I want to be forgiven
                and need to be (once in awhile).

I care about things,
    about getting them
        and being gotten by them;
And I do care about money
    and all the things I do for it,
        and with it,
            and what it does to me;
And I care about being a little freer
    of all that, somehow,
because I care about being secure
    core deep.

I care about my neighbors,
    at least some of them,
        sometimes;
and about all the things that would make it better,
    and perhaps easier
        for us to live together;
and the hard decisions and sacrifices
    it would take for that to happen.

Which means I do care about justice,
    though mostly from a distance,
        because I care about what it might require of me;
and then I get testy or silent
    but am haunted by it
because something in me
    won't let me stop caring about it,
        even though I often wish I could.

So, I care about my enemies,
     and am tired of being angry
          and suspicious so much,
               which is such a waste;
and I care about the least —
     the hungry
          and the sick
               and the terrorized
                    and the exploited of the earth —
because I care about peace
     and long for it inside and out,
          and am weary of being afraid
               for myself and the children.

I care about this tiny fragile blue planet,
     this home,
          this mother earth
               and all her offspring,
                    all the creatures who share
                         the mystery of life.
And I really do care about beauty,
     about the songs in me,
          the poems,
               the stories;
I care deeply about
     the wondrous,
          puzzling,
               aching struggle
                    that I am;
I care about this joy I feel
     flickering sometimes,
          flaring sometimes,
               when I touch hands
                    or eyes
                         or minds

           or sexes
             or souls,
and ache, then, for more.

I care about living —
    living more fully,
        abundantly —
           and about my urgent longing for that;
I care about what makes me restless,
    makes me reach
      and stretch
        and grope for words,
          for dreams,
            for other people,
             and . . .
               for you.

Holy One, you,
I do care about you,
    sometimes fiercely,
      or I wouldn't be stumbling along like this,
        trying to pray,
          trying to put myself in your way;
I care about you,
    and such is my faith,
      however faltering it is;
and I trust that, past words
    you care about all these things
      that I care about,
care about them more,
    infinitely more,
      than I care about them;
and that you care for me,
    even when I am careless
      of the things I care about.

There Is Something I Wanted to Tell You

Holy One,
there is something I wanted to tell you,
but there have been errands to run,
    bills to pay,
        arrangements to make,
            meetings to attend,
                friends to entertain,
                    washing to do . . .
and I forget what it is I wanted to say to you,
and mostly I forget what I'm about,
    or why.
O God,
don't forget me, please,
for the sake of Jesus Christ.

Eternal One,
there is something I wanted to tell you,
but my mind races with worrying and watching,
    with weighing and planning.
        with rutted slights and pothole grievances,
            with leaky dreams and leaky plumbing
                and leaky relationships I keep trying to plug up;
and my attention is preoccupied
    with loneliness,
        with doubt,
            and with things I covet;

and I forget what it is I wanted to say to you,
    and how to say it honestly
        or how to do much of anything.
O God,
don't forget me, please,
for the sake of Jesus Christ.

Almighty One,
there is something I wanted to ask you,
but I stumble along the edge of a nameless rage,
haunted by a hundred floating fears
    of nuclear war,
        of losing my job,
           of failing,
    of getting sick and old,
        of having loved ones die,
           of dying,
    of having no one love me,
        not even myself,
    and of not being sure who I am
        or that I am worth very much,
           and . . .
I forget what the real question is that I wanted to ask,
    and I forget to listen anyway
        because you seem unreal and far away,
and I forget what it is I have forgotten.
O God,
don't forget me, please,
for the sake of Jesus Christ.

O Father and Mother in Heaven,
perhaps you've already heard what I wanted to tell you.
What I wanted to ask is
    forgive me,
        heal me,
            increase my courage, please.
Renew in me a little of love and faith,
    and a sense of confidence,
        and a vision of what it might mean
            to live as though you were real,
                and I mattered,
                    and everyone was sister and brother.
What I wanted to ask in my blundering way is
    don't give up on me,
        don't become too sad about me,
            but laugh with me,
                and try again with me,
                    and I will with you, too.
What I wanted to ask is
    for peace enough to want and work for more,
        for joy enough to share,
            and for awareness that is keen enough
                to sense your presence
                  here,
                      now,
                        there,
                          then,
                            always.

I Remember Now in Silence

Lord,
plunge me deep into a sense of sadness
at the pain of my sisters and brothers
        inflicted by war,
                prejudice,
                        injustice,
                                indifference,
that I may learn again to cry as a child
until my tears baptize me
into a person who touches with care
those I now touch in prayer:
        victims of violence,
                of greed,
                        of addictions;
        prisoners in ghettos,
                in old age,
                        in sexism;
        people with broken bodies,
                with broken hearts,
                        with broken lives,
whom I remember now in silence before you
because I have too often forgotten them
in the shuffle of my fretful busy-ness.

Prayers for
Comfort & Reassurance

Sometimes It Just Seems to be Too Much

Sometimes, Lord,
it just seems to be too much:
    too much violence, too much fear;
    too much of demands and problems;
    too much of broken dreams and broken lives;
    too much of war and slums and dying;
    too much of greed and squishy fatness
        and the sounds of people
            devouring each other
                and the earth;
    too much of stale routines and quarrels,
        unpaid bills and dead ends;
    too much of words lobbed in to explode
        and leaving shredded hearts and lacerated souls;
    too much of turned-away backs and yellow silence,
        red rage and the bitter taste of ashes in my mouth.
Sometimes the very air seems scorched
    by threats and rejection and decay
        until there is nothing
            but to inhale pain
                and exhale confusion.
Too much of darkness, Lord,
    too much of cruelty
        and selfishness
            and indifference . . .

Too much, Lord,
    too much,
        too bloody,
            bruising,
                brain-washing much.

Or is it too little,
    too little of compassion,
too little of courage,
    of daring,
        of persistence,
            of sacrifice;
too little of music
    and laughter
        and celebration?

O God,
make of me some nourishment
    for these starved times,
some food
    for my brothers and sisters
        who are hungry for gladness and hope,
that, being bread for them,
    I may also be fed
        and be full.

God . . . Are You There?

God . . .
are you there?
I've been taught,
    and told I ought
        to pray.
But the doubt
    won't go away;
yet neither
    will my longing to be heard.
My soul sighs
    too deep for words.
Do you hear me?
God . . .
are you there?

Are you where love is?
I don't love well,
    or often,
        anything
            or anyone.
But, when I do,
    when I take the risk,
there's a sudden awareness
    of all I've missed;
and it's good,
    it's singing good.
For a moment
    life seems as it should.
But, I forget, so busy soon,
    that it was,
        or what
            or whom.
Help me!
God . . .
are you there?

How Shall I Pray?

How shall I pray?
    Are tears prayers, Lord?
    Are screams prayers,
        or groans
            or sighs
               or curses?
Can trembling hands be lifted to you,
    or clenched fists
        or the cold sweat that trickles down my back
            or the cramps that knot my stomach?
Will you accept my prayers, Lord,
    my real prayers,
        rooted in the muck and mud and rock of my life,
and not just my pretty, cut-flower, gracefully arranged
    bouquet of words?
Will you accept me, Lord,
    as I really am,
        messed up mixture of glory and grime?

Lord, help me!
Help me to trust that you do accept me as I am,
that I may be done with self-condemnation
    and self-pity,
        and accept myself.
Help me to accept you as you are, Lord:
    mysterious,
        hidden,
            strange,
               unknowable;
and yet to trust
    that your madness is wiser
        than my timid, self-seeking sanities,
and that nothing you've ever done
    has really been possible,
so I may dare to be a little mad, too.

Gather Me to Be with You

O God, gather me now
        to be with you
                as you are with me.
Soothe my tiredness;
        quiet my fretfulness;
                curb my aimlessness;
                        relieve my compulsiveness;
let me be easy for a moment.

O Lord, release me
        from the fears and guilts
                which grip me so tightly;
        from the expectations and opinions
                which I so tightly grip,
that I may be open
        to receiving what you give,
                to risking something genuinely new,
                        to learning something refreshingly different.

O God, gather me
        to be with you
                as you are with me.
Forgive me
        for claiming so much for myself
                that I leave no room for gratitude;
        for confusing exercises in self-importance
                with acceptance of self-worth;
        for complaining so much of my burdens
                that I become a burden;
        for competing against others so insidiously
                that I stifle celebrating them
                        and receiving your blessing through their gifts.

O God, gather me
      to be with you
            as you are with me.
Keep me in touch with myself,
      with my needs,
            my anxieties,
                  my angers,
                        my pains,
                              my corruptions,
that I may claim them as my own
rather than blame them on someone else.

O Lord, deepen my wounds
      into wisdom;
shape my weaknesses
      into compassion;
gentle my envy
      into enjoyment.
            my fear into trust,
                  my guilt into honesty,
                        my accusing fingers into tickling ones.

O God, gather me
      to be with you
            as you are with me.

I Want So to Belong

O God, I want so to belong;
    teach me to accept.
I want to be close;
    teach me to reach out.
I want a place where I am welcome;
    teach me to open my arms.
I want mercy;
    teach me to forgive.
I want beauty;
    teach me honesty.
I want peace;
    show me the eye of the storm.
I want truth;
    show me the way to question
        my unquestionable convictions.
I want joy;
    show me the way of deeper commitment.
I want life;
    show me how to die.

Breathe into Me

O God, empty me of angry judgments,
     and aching disappointments,
        and anxious trying,
and breathe into me
     something like quietness
        and confidence,
that the lion and the lamb in me
     may lie down together
        and be led by a trust
as straightforward as a little child.

Catch my pride and doubt off guard
that, at least for the moment,
I may sense your presence
     and your caring,
and be surprised
     by a sudden joy
        rising in me now
to sustain me in the coming then.

I Have So Few Ways to Pray

Lord,
I have so few ways to pray,
    but you have so many ways to answer.
Keep me alert
      to your unpredictable answers,
         to your unexplainable surprises,
and by your grace,
make me one of those surprises,
for the sake of the One
      who taught us the surprises
         of moving mountains,
            healing touches,
               wondrous stories,
                  great banquets,
                     first suppers,
                        broken bread,
                          crosses,
                            and resurrections.

Give Me Hope

O God,
this is a hard time,
a season of confusion,
    a frantic rush
        to fill my closets,
           my schedule,
             and my mind,
only to find myself empty.

Give me hope, Lord,
and remind me
    of your steady power
        and gracious purposes
that I may live fully.
Renew my faith
    that the earth is not destined
        for dust and darkness,
    but for frolicking life
        and deep joy
that, being set free
    from my anxiety for the future,
I may take the risks of love
    today.

Waken in Me a Gratitude for My Life

O God, complete the work you have begun in me.
Release through me
    a flow of mercy and gentleness that will bring
    water where there is desert,
    healing where there is hurt,
    peace where there is violence,
    beauty where there is ugliness,
    justice where there is brokenness,
    beginnings where there are dead-ends.
Waken in me
    gratitude for my life,
    love for every living thing,
    joy in what is human and holy,
    praise for you.
Renew my faith that you are God
    beyond my grasp
        but within my reach;
    past my knowing
        but within my searching;
    disturber of the assured,
        assurer of the disturbed;
    destroyer of illusions,
        creator of dreams;
    source of silence and music,
        sex and solitude,
            light and darkness,
                death and life.
O Keeper of Promises,
    composer of grace,
grant me
    glee in my blood,
        prayer in my heart,
            trust at my core,
                songs for my journey,
                    and a sense of your kingdom.

I Teeter on the Brink of Endings

O God of endings,
    you promised to be with me always,
        even to the end of time.
Move with me now in these occasions of last things,
    of shivering vulnerabilities and letting go:
        letting go of parents gone,
            past gone,
                friends going,
                    old self growing;
        letting go of children grown,
            needs outgrown,
                prejudices ingrown,
                    illusions overgrown;
        letting go of swollen grudges and shrunken loves.
Be with me in my end of things,
my letting go of dead things,
    dead ways,
        dead words,
            dead self I hold so tightly,
                defend so blindly,
                    fear losing so frantically.
I teeter on the brink of endings:
    some anticipated,
        some resisted,
            some inevitable,
                some surprising,
                    most painful;
and the mystery of them quiets me to awe.
In silence, Lord,
I feel now the curious blend of grief and gladness in me
over the endings that the ticking and whirling of things brings;
and I listen for your leading
    to help me faithfully move on through the fear
        of my time to let go
            so the timeless may take hold of me.

Prayers for
Restoration & Renewal

I Am in Need of . . . of What?

Well, God,
I made it through another sweet-sour time,
and here I am,
    nibbled,
        frazzled,
            puzzled,
                awed,
and in need of . . . of what?
    A chuckle, maybe,
        a revolution begun with a belly laugh,
            a Bronx cheer in the face of the onslaughts
                of disaster and death itself.
Such is my need;
and this is my wonder:
    Are you really as humorless,
        as grimly serious
            as I have made you out to be?
    Or do aardvarks and monkeys,
        bull frogs and platypuses,
            puppies and porpoises,
                and people, perhaps,
    reveal the comic side of your grace,
        the playful side of your love?
Tickle me into giggling down
    the wailing walls
        of my endless grievances.
and trip up my waddling pomposities.

Lord of laughter, as of tears,
shake me awake
and teach me to laugh at myself,
    at my black-draped solemnity,
        over my petty preoccupation with success and failure,
            through all the hurt and adversity
until my laughter lures me deep
    beneath the terrors without names,
        beneath the questions without answers,
            beneath the pain without relief;
lures me deep
    to the love in me unused,
        to the strength unspent,
            to the courage untapped,
                to the dream unrisked,
                    to the beauty unexpressed;
all the way down
    to the inescapable bottom,
        to the awareness that I must get on
            with being who I am
                as fully as I can,
                    as unflinchingly as I can,
                        as accurately as I can,
which is to say,
    as gracefully,
        as powerfully,
            as faithfully
as you have created me to be.

Touch Me Deeply so that I Will Find a Sense of Self

O Ingenious God,
I rejoice in your creation,
and pray that your Spirit touch me so deeply
that I will find a sense of self
     which makes me glad to be who I am
        and yet restless
           at being anything less
             than I can become.
Make me simple enough
     not to be confused by disappointments,
clear enough
     not to mistake busyness for freedom,
honest enough
     not to expect truth to be painless,
brave enough
     not to sing all my songs in private,
compassionate enough
     to get in trouble,
humble enough
     to admit trouble and seek help,
joyful enough
     to celebrate all of it,
        myself and others and you
through Jesus Christ our Lord.

Draw Me to Yourself

In this moment
draw me to yourself, Lord,
and make me aware
    not so much of what I've given
        as of all I have received
           and so have yet to share.
Send me forth
    in power and gladness
        and with great courage
           to live out in the world
               what I pray and profess,
that, in sharing,
    I may do justice,
        make peace,
           grow in love,
               enjoy myself,
                  other people,
                    and your world now,
                    and you forever.

Help Me Unbury Wonder

O God of the miracles,
        of galaxies
                and crocuses
                        and children,
I praise you now
        from the soul of the child within me,
                shy in my awe,
                        delighted by my foolishness,
                                stubborn in my wanting,
                                        persistent in my questioning,
                                                and bold in my asking you
to help me unbury my talents
        for wonder
                and humor
                        and gratitude,
so I may invest them eagerly
        in the recurring mysteries
                of spring and beginnings,
                        of willows that weep,
                                and rivers that flow
                                        and people who grow
in such endlessly amazing
        and often painful ways;
that I will be forever linked and loyal
        to justice and joy,
                simplicity and humanity,
                        Christ and his kingdom.

Let Wonder Have Its Way with Me

O God, your gracious Spirit
moves over the mysteries of living and dying
and is strangely present to me
    in the falling leaves,
        the call of the wild geese,
           a child's birth,
              the light in a friend's eyes,
                  the sudden lifting of the heart,
                     and the deep longing which brings me to you now.
Make me aware of your presence
that wonder may have its way with me,
    my passion be released,
        my confidence renewed in the depths of your holiness
until, for a moment,
my longing for you be fulfilled
and I know I am really free
    to share bread and intimacy,
        to laugh and exchange mercy,
           to be at ease in my struggles,
              bold in my loving,
                brave in facing down my terror,
                  hopeful in the rising music of your kingdom,
                    joyful in my living,
                     and graceful in my life becoming
                       a song of praise ever sung to you.

Let Something Essential Happen to Me

O God,
let something essential happen to me,
    something more than interesting
        or entertaining,
           or thoughtful.
O God,
let something essential happen to me,
    something awesome,
        something real.
Speak to my condition, Lord,
and change me somewhere inside where it matters,
a change that will burn and tremble and heal
    and explode me into tears
        or laughter
           or love that throbs or screams
              or keeps a terrible, cleansing silence
                and dares the dangerous deeds.
Let something happen in me
which is my real self, God.

O God,
let something essential and passionate happen in me now.
Strip me of my illusions of self-sufficiency,
    of my proud sophistications,
        of my inflated assumptions of knowledge
and leave me shivering as Adam or Eve
    before the miracle of the natural —
        the miracle of this earth
           that nurtures me as a mother
             and delights me as a lover;

the miracle of my body
    that breathes and moves,
        hungers and digests,
            sees and hears;
    that is creased and wrinkled and sexual,
        shrinks in hurt,
            and swells in pleasure;
    that works by the most amazing messages
        of what and when and how,
            coded and curled in every cell
    and that dares to speak the confronting word.

O God,
let something essential and joyful happen in me now.
something like the blooming of hope and faith,
    like a grateful heart,
        like a surge of awareness
            of how precious each moment is,
that now, not next time,
now is the occasion
    to take off my shoes,
        to see every bush afire,
            to leap and whirl with neighbor,
                to gulp the air as sweet wine
until I've drunk enough
    to dare to speak the tender word:
        "Thank you";
            "I love you";
                "You're beautiful";
                    "Let's live forever beginning now";
                        and "I'm a fool for Christ's sake."

Touch Me

Come, Lord Jesus,
touch me
    with love, life-giving as light,
to quiet my anger a little,
    and gentle my desperation,
to soften my fears some
    and soothe the knots of my cynicism,
to wipe away the tears from my eyes
    and ease the pains in my body and soul,
to reconcile me to myself
    and then to the people around me,
        and then nation to nation,
that none shall learn war any more,
    but turn to feed the hungry,
        house the homeless
           and care compassionately
              for the least of our brothers and sisters.
Reshape me in your wholeness
to be a healing person, Lord.

Come, Lord Jesus,
expand me
    by your power, life-generating as the sea,
to accept
    and use my power,
to do something I believe in
    and be something more of who I mean to be
        and can be,
to inspire me to dream and move,
    sweat and sing,
        fail and laugh,
           cuss and create,
to link my passion with courage,
    my hope with discipline,
        my love with persistence,

to enable me to learn from difficulties,
    grow in adversities,
        gain wisdom from defeats,
            perspective from disappointments,
                gracefulness from crises,
    and find joy
        in simply living it all fully.
Release me through your power
to be a powerful person, Lord.

Come, Lord Jesus,
startle me
    with your presence, life-sustaining as air,
to open my heart
    to praise you,
to open my mind
    to attend you,
to open my spirit
    to worship you,
to open me
    to live my life
        as authentically and boldly
            as you lived yours.

Come, Lord Jesus,
be with me
    in my longing;
come, stay with me
    in my needing;
come, go with me
    in my doing;
come, struggle with me
    in my searching;
come, rejoice with me
    in my loving.

Keep Me in Touch with My Dreams

O Lord,
in the turbulence
    and the loneliness
        of my living from day to day
          and night to night,
keep me in touch with my roots,
    so I will remember where I came from
      and with whom;
keep me in touch with my feelings,
    so I will be more aware of who I really am
      and what it costs;
keep me in touch with my mind
    so I will know who I am not
      and what that means;
and keep me in touch with my dreams,
    so I will grow toward where I want to go
      and for whom.

O Lord,
deliver me
    from the arrogance of assuming
      I know enough to judge others;
deliver me
    from the timidity of presuming
      I don't know enough to help others;
deliver me
    from the illusion of claiming I have changed enough
      when I have only risked little,
that, so liberated,
    I will make some of the days to come different.

O Lord,
I ask not to be delivered
    from the tensions that wind me tight,
but I do ask for
    a sense of direction in which to move once wound,
        a sense of humor about my disappointments,
            a sense of respect for the elegant puzzlement of being human,
                and a sense of gladness for your kingdom
                    which comes in spite of my fretful pulling and tugging.

O Lord,
nurture in me
    the song of a lover,
        the vision of a poet,
            the questions of a child,
                the boldness of a prophet,
                    the courage of a disciple.

O Lord,
it is said you created people
    because you love stories.
Be with me as I live out my story.

Quicken in Me a Sense of Humor

O God of gifts,
quicken in me a sense of humor
  bright enough to help me find my way
    in these tarnished times,
  fruitful enough to be made the wine of hope
    to warm the hearts of those I live with.
Make me glad to be one of a kind,
  yet one with a kind,
    called not to be more like others,
      but more of myself,
        a guerrilla of grace,
          that, in daring to be authentic,
           I may become more of a human-kind.

So, O God of gifts,
liberate me to share,
  without apology or arrogance,
    not only the gifts I have,
      but the gift I am.

Set Me Free

Lord of wondrous patience,
the earth has risen again,
emerging
    from a darkness
        in a way it has never quite been before;
whirling
    to a fresh time,
        an unused space;
alive
    with trembling possibilities,
        and I with it!
Such staggering grace!
Please,
nurture me in newness;
set me free from the tyrannies
    of habit
        and complaining
            and blaming;
shake from me the dusty melancholy
    of too much success and comfort,
        pride and pretense,
that, as if on the first day of creation,
I may begin to see
    the miracle of life and humanity;
to hear
    the hum of grace
        unfolding to meet all my needs,
            unexpectedly and surprisingly,
                and urging me to go on in faith
                    to whatever is next in love.

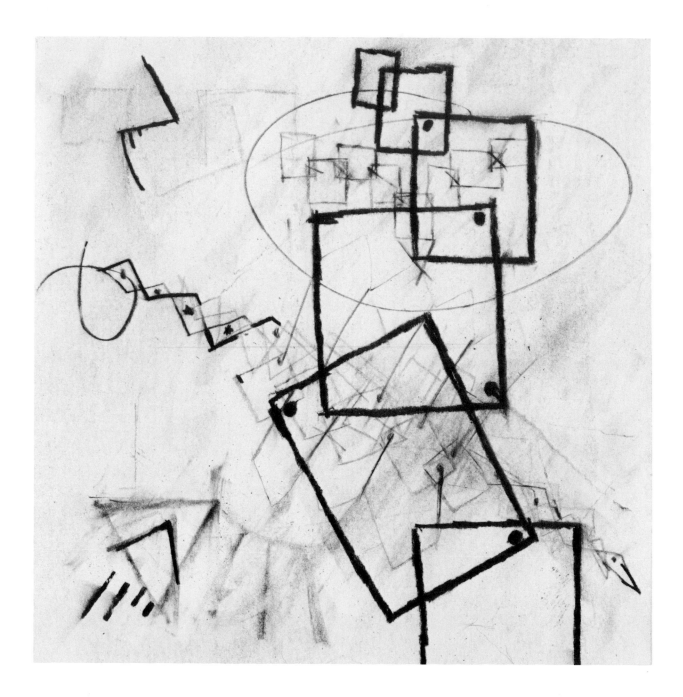

Prayers of
Commitment & Change

Pry Me off Dead Center

O persistent God,
deliver me from assuming your mercy is gentle.
Pressure me that I may grow more human,
    not through the lessening of my struggles,
    but through an expansion of them
    that will undamn me
    and unbury my gifts.
Deepen my hurt
    until I learn to share it
    and myself
    openly,
    and my needs honestly.
Sharpen my fears
    until I name them
    and release the power I have locked in them
    and they in me.
Accentuate my confusion
    until I shed those grandiose expectations
    that divert me from the small, glad gifts
    of the now and the here and the me.
Expose my shame where it shivers,
    crouched behind the curtains of propriety,
    until I can laugh at last
    through my common frailities and failures,
    laugh my way toward becoming whole.

Deliver me
     from just going through the motions
     and wasting everything I have
     which is today,
        a chance,
           a choice,
              my creativity,
                 your call.

O persistent God,
let how much it all matters
pry me off dead center
so if I am moved inside
     to tears
        or sighs
           or screams
              or smiles
                 or dreams,
they will be real
and I will be in touch with who I am
and who you are
and who my sisters and brothers are.

Help Me to Believe in Beginnings

God of history and of my heart,
so much has happened to me during these whirlwind days:
    I've known death and birth;
    I've been brave and scared;
    I've hurt, I've helped;
    I've been honest, I've lied;
    I've destroyed, I've created;
    I've been with people, I've been lonely;
    I've been loyal, I've betrayed;
    I've decided, I've waffled;
    I've laughed and I've cried.
You know my frail heart and my frayed history —
and now another day begins.

O God, help me to believe in beginnings
and in my beginning again,
no matter how often I've failed before.

Help me to make beginnings:
    to begin going out of my weary mind
        into fresh dreams,
            daring to make my own bold tracks
                in the land of now;
    to begin forgiving
        that I may experience mercy;
    to begin questioning the unquestionable
        that I may know truth;
    to begin disciplining
        that I may create beauty;
    to begin sacrificing
        that I may accomplish justice;
    to begin risking
        that I may make peace;
    to begin loving
        that I may realize joy.

Help me to be a beginning for others,
  to be a singer to the songless,
  a storyteller to the aimless,
  a befriender of the friendless;
to become a beginning of hope for the despairing,
  of assurance for the doubting,
  of reconciliation for the divided;
to become a beginning of freedom for the oppressed,
  of comfort for the sorrowing,
  of friendship for the forgotten;
to become a beginning of beauty for the forlorn,
  of sweetness for the soured,
  of gentleness for the angry,
  of wholeness for the broken,
  of peace for the frightened and violent of the earth.

Help me to believe in beginnings,
  to make a beginning,
   to be a beginning,
so that I may not just grow old,
  but grow new
each day of this wild, amazing life
  you call me to live
   with the passion of Jesus Christ.

Breathe into Me the Courage to Make Something New

Thank you for all I forget are gifts,
  not rights.
Forgive me for all the grievances
  I remember too well.
Save me from the self-pity,
    the self-seeking,
        the fat-heartedness
            which is true poverty.
Guide me, if I'm willing,
    (drive me if I'm not),
        into the hard ways of sacrifice
            which are just and loving.
Make me wide-eyed for beauty,
    and for my neighbor's need and goodness;
wide-willed for peace-making,
    and for the confronting power
        with the call to compassion;
wide-hearted for love
    and for the unloved,
        who are the hardest to touch
            and need it the most.

Dull the envy in me
    which criticizes and complains life
        into a thousand ugly bits.
Keep me honest and tender enough to heal,
    tough enough to be healed of my hypocrisies.
Match my appetite for privilege
    with the stomach for commitment.
Teach me the great cost of paying attention
    that, naked to the dazzle of your back as you pass,
        I may know I am always on holy ground.
Breathe into me the restlessness and courage
    to make something new,
        something saving,
            and something true
that I may understand what it is to rejoice.

Teach Me Your Ways

Teach me your ways, Lord,
    that I may be open to the same Spirit
        who moved over the face of the waters
            in the first day of creation
        and moves also over the chaos of this time
            to fashion a day like this,
                a world like ours,
                    a life like mine,
                        a kingdom like leaven in bread,
                        like a treasure
                                buried in the fields of the daily I plow;
and make me aware of the miracles of life,
    of warm and cold,
        of starkness and order,
            of screaming wind and impenetrable silences,
                and of the unfathomable mystery of amazing grace in which I am kept.

Teach me your ways, Lord,
    that I may praise you
        for all the surprising, ingenious ways you bless me,
            and for all the wondrous gifts you give me
                through artists who introduce me to the beauty of holiness,
                    who usher me into awesome worlds in which I begin to live anew
                    in a fullness of pain and joy not possible before.

Teach me your ways, Lord,
    that I may accept my own talent openly,
        nurture it hopefully,
           develop it faithfully,
              and give it freely.

Teach me your ways, Lord,
    that I may love the kindness of the prophets
        and practice it toward the hungry of the world,
           the poor and sick and oppressed
    that I may learn the healing humility
        which responsibly tends the earth and all creatures therein.

Teach me your ways, Lord,
    that I may be swept up in worship with the saints,
        which surges in wonder, gratitude and obedience,
           and shapes my life into an irrepressible YES to you,
              to all my sisters and brothers,
                and to the presence of the kingdom among us
  until the ancient vision of mothers burns in me
        with a fire to light the world
        and warm its heart,
           through Jesus Christ,
              the singer of passionate songs,
                the teller of powerful stories,
                  the artist of daring ways.

I Claim Your Power to Create

O Ingenious One,
it is not only creation,
    but creativity
        that awes me.
It is a wondrous,
    fearsome thing
        that you share your power to create.

O Mysterious One,
I shrink from your power,
    yet I claim it;
        and it is mine by your genius
           or madness,
this power to speak
    and have light burst upon a mind
        or darkness descend upon a heart;
this power to make music
    to which souls dance
        or armies march;
this power to mold and paint and carve
    and so spin out the stars
        by which I plot my course to heaven or to hell;
this power to hear and touch and taste
    the love and truth
        by which life itself is birthed and built,
           or the hate and lies
               by which it shrivels and dies.

O Daring One,
it is an awesome power you've shared;
and I rejoice in the artists
    who dare to use their gift
        to create the beauty which casts this world
           into a more whole and holy dimension,

who dare to breathe visions and vibrations
into dullness,
as you breathed life into dust.

O Gracious One,
it is an awesome power you've shared;
and I honor your power
not only in pianist, poet and painter,
but in those whose encouragement ignites my heart,
whose laughter lights up a room,
whose touch fills a void,
whose integrity inspires my will,
whose commitment builds a church,
whose compassion builds a community,
whose demands stretch my soul,
and whose love makes my day;
and I honor your power in those artists
of kitchen and office and shop,
of courtroom and classroom and sickroom;
in those crazy people
who somehow know the world is always unfinished,
and who happily risk pushing and shoving
and tugging and pounding
and making love to it
until it and all of us
come out in more glorious shape.

O Ingenious One,
it is not only creation,
but creativity
that awes me.
It is a wondrous,
fearsome thing
that you share your power to create.

Turn Your Spirit Loose

O God,
turn your Spirit loose now,
    and me with it,
that I may go to where the edge is
    to face with you the shape of my mortality:
        the inescapable struggle
            and loneliness and pain
                which remind me
                    that I am less than god after all,
                        that you have made me with hard limits,
                      limits to my strength,
                        my knowledge,
                          my days.

Facing those limits, Lord,
grant me grace
    to live to the limit
        of being unflinchingly alive,
            irrepressibly alive,
                fully alive,
        of experiencing
            every fragile,
                miraculous,
                    bloody,
                      juicy,
                        aching,
                          beautiful ounce
                          of being a human being;
    of doing my duty
        and a little more;
    of loving the people around me,
        my friends and my enemies;
    of humbling myself to take others seriously
        and delightedly;
    of applying my heart to the wisdom of simplicity,
        the freedom of honesty.

O God,
turn your Spirit loose here,
    and me with it,
that I may go to where the silence is
    to face with you the utter mystery
        of questions without answers,
            pain without balm,
                sorrow without comfort,
                    and fears without relief,
                        which hound my days
                            and haunt my sleep.
Facing the mystery, Lord,
grant me grace
    to wrestle with it
        until I name the fears
            and force them to set me free
                to move on with whatever limp I'm left with;
    to wrestle with it
        until the pain teach me
        and I befriend it,
    until the silence subdues me
        into an awareness that it is holy
        and I am healed by it;
    to wrestle with it
        until I go deeper in it
            to gratitude
                for all the shapes of wholeness
                    and of hope that bless me.

O God,
turn your Spirit loose now,
 and me with it,
that I may go to where the darkness is
 to face with you the terrible uncertainty of tomorrow:
  of what will happen,
   what might happen,
    what could happen,
     to me
      and to my children
       and to my friends,
     to my job,
      to my relationships,
       to my country;
   all that I cannot see, but fantasize,
    that I would prevent, but cannot,
     and so must accept as possibilities.
Facing the uncertainty, Lord,
grant me grace
 to look at it directly and openly and truly,
 to laugh at it with crazy faith
  in the crazy promise
   that nothing can separate me from your love;
 to laugh for the joy of it,
  the joy of those saving surprises
   that also stir in the darkness.
And, so, I trust,
 despite the dark uncertainty of tomorrow,
  in the light of my todays,
   in the cross,
    and in a kingdom coming,
and, so, I move on and pray on
with Jesus, my friend and redeemer.

Bring More of What I Dream

O God,
who out of nothing
    brought everything that is,
out of what I am
    bring more of what I dream
        but haven't dared;
direct my power and passion
    to creating life
        where there is death,
    to putting flesh of action
        on bare-boned intentions,
    to lighting fires
        against the midnight of indifference,
    to throwing bridges of care
        across canyons of loneliness;
so I can look on creation,
    together with you,
        and, behold,
            call it very good;
through Jesus Christ my Lord.

I Tremble on the Edge of a Maybe

O God of beginnings,
as your Spirit moved
    over the face of the deep
        on the first day of creation,
move with me now
    in my time of beginnings,
        when the air is rain-washed.
           the bloom is on the bush,
               and the world seems fresh
                  and full of possibilities,
                     and I feel ready and full.

I tremble on the edge of a maybe,
    a first time,
        a new thing,
           a tentative start,
and the wonder of it lays its finger on my lips.

In silence, Lord,
I share now my eagerness
    and my uneasiness
        about this something different
           I would be or do;
and I listen for your leading
    to help me separate the light
        from the darkness
           in the change I seek to shape
              and which is shaping me.

Go with Me in a New Exodus

O God of fire and freedom,
deliver me from my bondage
    to what can be counted
and go with me in a new exodus
    toward what counts,
but can only be measured
    in bread shared
        and swords become plowshares;
    in bodies healed
        and minds liberated;
    in songs sung
        and justice done;
    in laughter in the night
        and joy in the morning;
    in love through all seasons
        and great gladness of heart;
    in all people coming together
        and a kingdom coming in glory;
    in your name being praised
        and my becoming an alleluia,
through Jesus the Christ.

Prayers for
Seasons & Holidays

I Hold My Life Up to You Now

Patient God,
the clock struck midnight
        and I partied with a strange sadness in my heart,
                confusion in my mind.
Now, I ask you
        to gather me,
                for I realize
                        the storms of time have scattered me,
                                the furies of the year past have driven me,
                                many sorrows have scarred me,
                        many accomplishments have disappointed me,
                        much activity has wearied me,
                                and fear has spooked me
                                        into a hundred hiding places,
                                                one of which is pretended gaiety.
I am sick of a string of "Have a nice day's."
What I want is passionate days,
        wondrous days,
                dangerous days,
                        blessed days,
                                surprising days.
What I want is you!

Patient God,
this day teeters on the edge of waiting
    and things seem to slip away from me,
        as though everything was only memory
          and memory is capricious.
Help me not to let my life slip away from me.
O God, I hold up my life to you now,
    as much as I can,
        as high as I can,
          in this mysterious reach called prayer.
Come close, lest I wobble and fall short.
It is not days or years I seek from you,
    not infinity and enormity,
        but small things and moments and awareness,
          awareness that you are in what I am
            and in what I have been indifferent to.
It is not new time,
    but new eyes,
        new heart I seek,
          and you.

Patient God,
in this teetering time,
        this time in the balance,
                this time of waiting,
make me aware of moments,
        moments of song,
                moments of bread and friends,
                        moments of jokes
                                (some of them on me)
                                        which, for a moment, deflate my pomposities;
moments of sleep and warm beds,
        moments of children laughing and parents bending,
                moments of sunsets and sparrows outspunking winter,
moments when broken things get mended
        with glue or guts or mercy or imagination;
                moments when splinters shine and rocks shrink,
                moments when I know myself blest,
                        not because I am so awfully important,
                                but because you are so awesomely God,
                                        no less of the year to come
                                                as of all the years past;
                                        no less of this moment
                                                than of all my moments;
                                        no less of those who forget you
                                                as of those who remember,
                                                        as I do now,
                                                                in this teetering time.

O Patient God,
make something new in me,
        in this year,
                for you.

Catch Me in My Scurrying

Catch me in my anxious scurrying, Lord,
and hold me in this Lenten season:
hold my feet to the fire of your grace
    and make me attentive to my mortality
        that I may begin to die now
           to those things that keep me
               from living with you
                  and with my neighbors on this earth;
        to grudges and indifference,
           to certainties that smother possibilities,
              to my fascination with false securities,
                to my addiction to sweatless dreams,
                  to my arrogant insistence on how it has to be;
        to my corrosive fear of dying someday
           which eats away the wonder of living this day,
              and the adventure of losing my life
                in order to find it in you.

Catch me in my aimless scurrying, Lord,
and hold me in this Lenten season:
hold my heart to the beat of your grace
    and create in me a resting place,
        a kneeling place,
           a tip-toe place

where I can recover from the dis-ease of my grandiosities
    which fill my mind and calendar with busy self-importance,
that I may become vulnerable enough
    to dare intimacy with the familiar,
        to listen cup-eared for your summons,
            and to watch squint-eyed for your crooked finger
                in the crying of a child,
                    in the hunger of the street people,
                        in the fear of nuclear holocaust in all people,
                in the rage of those oppressed because of sex or race,
                  in the smoldering resentments of exploited third world nations,
                    in the sullen apathy of the poor and ghetto-strangled people,
                  in my lonely doubt and limping ambivalence;

and somehow,
    during this season of sacrifice,
        enable me to sacrifice time
        and possessions
            and securities,
to do something . . .
    something about what I see,
        something to turn the water of my words
            into the wine of will and risk,
                into the bread of blood and blisters,
                into the blessedness of deed,
            of a cross picked up,
                a saviour followed.

Catch me in my mindless scurrying, Lord,
and hold me in this Lenten season:
hold my spirit to the beacon of your grace
    and grant me light enough to walk boldly,
        to feel passionately,
            to love aggressively;
grant me peace enough to want more,
    to work for more
        and to submit to nothing less,
           and to fear only you . . .
              only you!

4

Give ~~Bequeath~~ me not becalmed seas,
    slack sails and premature benedictions,
        but breathe into me a torment,
          storm enough to make within myself
          and from myself,
            something . . .

5

something new,
    something saving,
      something true,
a gladness of heart,
    a pitch for a song in the storm,
      a word of praise lived,
        a gratitude shared,
          a cross dared,
            a joy received.

Be with Me in My Unfolding

It is spring, Lord,
and the land is coming up green again,
    unfolding
        outside my well-drawn boundaries
           and urgent schedules.
And there is the mystery
    and the smile of it.
The willows are dripping honey color into the rivers,
and the mother birds are busy in manger nests,
and I am learning again
    that "for everything there is a season
        and a time for every matter under heaven."
O Lord, you have sketched the lines of spring.
Be with me in my unfolding.

It is spring, Lord,
and my blood runs warm with the song of the sap,
    longing
        for a beauty I would become.
And there is the mystery
    and the smile of it.
The buds are swelling on the bush,
    the sun is beginning to coax the color
        from where it's been curled against the cold,
          the air is sweet to the nostrils;
even the city seems to be rubbing its eyes
    from a long sleep;

and there is a promise in the season
        I know no name for
                except life.
O Lord, you have sketched the lines of spring.
Be with me in my longing.

It is spring, Lord,
and something stirs in me,
        reaching, stretching,
                groping for words,
                        peeking through my defenses,
                                beckoning in my laughter,
                                        riding on past my fears,
                                                pulsing in my music.
And there is the mystery
        and the smile of it.
Be with me in my reaching
        so I will touch or be touched,
                this time,
                        by a grace, a warmth, a light,
        to unfold my life to a new beginning,
                a fresh budding,
                        a spring within as well as around me.
O Lord, you have sketched the lines of spring.
Be with me in my reaching.

Shock Me with the Terrible Goodness of this Friday

Holy one,
shock and save me with the terrible goodness of this Friday,
and drive me deep into my longing for your kingdom,
until I seek it first —
    yet not first for myself,
but for the hungry
    and the sick
       and the poor of your children,
for prisoners of conscience around the world,
for those I have wasted
    with my racism
      and sexism
        and ageism
          and nationalism
           and religionism,
for those around this mother earth and in this city
who, this Friday, know far more of terror than of goodness;
that, in my seeking first the kingdom,
    for them as well as for myself,
      all these things may be mine as well:
things like a coat and courage
    and something like comfort,
      a few lilies in the field,
        the sight of birds soaring on the wind,
          a song in the night,
           and gladness of heart,
the sense of your presence
    and the realization of your promise
      that nothing in life or death
        will be able to separate me or those I love,
          from your love
           in the crucified one who is our Lord,
            and in whose name and Spirit I pray.

I Praise You for this Resurrection Madness

Lord of such amazing surprises
     as put a catch in my breath
        and wings on my heart,
I praise you for this joy,
     too great for words,
        but not for tears and songs and sharing;
     for this mercy
        that blots out my betrayals
           and bids me begin again,
              to limp on,
                to hop-skip-and-jump on,
                  to mend what is broken
                    in and around me,
                      and to forgive the breakers;
     for this YES
        to life and laughter,
          to love and lovers,
            and to my unwinding self;
     for this kingdom
        unleashed in me and I in it forever,
        and no dead ends to growing,
          to choices,
            to chances,
              to calls to be just;
     no dead ends to living,
        to making peace,
          to dreaming dreams,
            to being glad of heart;
     for this resurrection madness
        which is wiser than I
        and in which I see
          how great you are,
            how full of grace.
             Alleluia!

Touch Me with Truth that Burns Like Fire

Lord,
send the gift of your Spirit
    to fill this place
        and myself
           and the world.
Touch me
    with truth
        that burns like fire,
          with beauty
            that moves me like the wind;
and set me free, Lord,
    free to try new ways of living;
        free to forgive myself and others;
          free to love and laugh and sing;
            free to lay aside my burden of security;
              free to join the battle for justice and peace;
               free to see and listen and wonder again
                  at the gracious mystery of things and persons;
free to be,
    to give,
      to receive,
        to rejoice as a child of your Spirit.

And, Lord,
teach me how to dance,
    to turn around
        and come down where I want to be,
          in the arms and heart of your people
          and in you,
that I may praise and enjoy you forever.

Let Me Live Grace-fully

Thank you, Lord,
for this season
    of sun and slow motion,
        of games and porch sitting,
            of picnics and light green fireflies
                on heavy purple evenings;
and praise for slight breezes.
It's good, God,
as the first long days of your creation.

Let this season be for me
    a time of gathering together the pieces
        into which my busyness has broken me.
O God, enable me now
    to grow wise through reflection,
        peaceful through the song of the cricket,
            recreated through the laughter of play.

Most of all, Lord,
let me live easily and grace-fully for a spell,
    so that I may see other souls deeply,
        share in a silence unhurried,
           listen to the sound of sunlight and shadows,
                explore barefoot the land of forgotten dreams and shy hopes,
                  and find the right words to tell another who I am.

Waken in Me a Sense of Joy

O extravagant God,
in this ripening, red-tinged autumn,
waken in me a sense of joy
        in just being alive,
joy for nothing in general
        except everything in particular;
joy in sun and rain
        mating with earth to birth a harvest;
joy in soft light
        through shyly disrobing trees;
joy in the acolyte moon
        setting halos around processing clouds;
joy in the beating of a thousand wings
        mysteriously knowing which way is warm;
joy in wagging tails and kids' smiles
        and in this spunky old city;
joy in the taste of bread and wine,
        the smell of dawn,
                a touch,
                        a song,
                                a presence;
joy in having what I cannot live without —
        other people to hold and cry and laugh with;
joy in love,
        in you;
and that all at first and last
is grace.

My Words Can't Carry All the Praise

Glorious God,
how curious
    and what a confession
        that we should set aside one day a year
           and call it Thanksgiving.
I smile at the presumption,
    and hope you smile, too.
But the truth is,
    Holy Friend,
        that my words can't carry all the praise
           I want them to,
               or that they should,
                  no matter how many trips they make.

So this day,
    all is praise and thanks
        for all my days.
I breathe and it is your breath that fills me.
    I look and it is your light by which I see.
        I move and it is your energy moving in me.
I listen and even the stones speak of you.
    I touch and you are between finger and skin.
        I think and the thoughts are but sparks
           from the fire of your truth.
I love and the throb is your presence.
    I laugh and it is the rustle of your passing.

I weep and your Spirit broods over me.
　　I long and it is the tug of your kingdom.

I praise you, Glorious One,
for what has been, and is and will ever be:
for galaxy upon galaxy, mass and energy,
　　earth and air, sun and night,
　　　　sea and shore, mountain and valley,
　　　　　　root and branch, male and female,
creature upon creature in a thousand ingenious ways,
　　two-legged, hundred-legged, smooth, furry, and feathery,
　　　　bull-frogs and platypuses, peacocks and preachers,
and the giggle of it—
　　and turkeys (especially, this day, the roasted kind, not the flops)—
　　　　and families gathered, and the thanking;
　　　　　　the brave, lonely one, and the asking;
　　　　　　　　the growling, hungry ones, and the sharing.

I praise you, Glorious One,
for this color splashed, memory haunted,
　　hope filled, justice seeking,
　　　　love grown country
and the labors that birthed it,
　　the dreams that nurtured it,
　　　　the riches that sometimes misguide it,
　　　　　　the sacrifices that await it,
　　　　　　　　the destiny that summons it
　　　　　　　　　　to become a blessing to the whole human family!

O Glorious One,
for this curious day,
        for the impulses that have designated it,
            for the gifts that grace it,
                for the gladness that accompanies it,
for my life,
        for those through whom I came to be,
            for friends through whom I hear and see
                greater worlds than otherwise I would,
for all the doors of words and music and worship
        through which I pass to larger worlds,
            and for the One who brought a kingdom to me,
I pause to praise and thank you
        with this one more trip of words
            which leaves too much uncarried,
                but not unfelt,
                    unlived,
                        unloved.
                            Thank you!

Grant Me Your Sense of Timing

O God of all seasons and senses,
grant me your sense of timing
    to submit gracefully
        and rejoice quietly
            in the turn of the seasons.

In this season of short days and long nights,
    of grey and white and cold,
teach me the lessons of waiting:
    of the snow joining the mystery
        of the hunkered-down seeds
           growing in their sleep
                watched over by gnarled-limbed, grandparent trees
                    resting from autumn's staggering energy;
                of the silent, whirling earth
                    circling to race back home to the sun.
O God, grant me your sense of timing.

In this season of short days and long nights,
    of grey and white and cold,
teach me the lessons of endings:
    children growing,
        friends leaving,

jobs concluding,
        stages finishing,
            grieving over,
                grudges over,
                    blaming over,
                        excuses over.
O God, grant me your sense of timing.

In this season of short days and long nights,
        of grey and white and cold,
teach me the lessons of beginnings:
        that such waitings and endings
            may be a starting place,
                a planting of seeds
                    which bring to birth
                        what is ready to be born —
                            something right and just and different,
                                a new song,
                                    a deeper relationship,
                                        a fuller love—
                                            in the fullness of your time.
O God, grant me your sense of timing.

I Am Silent . . . and Expectant

How silently,
how silently
the wondrous gift is given.

I would be silent now,
Lord,
and expectant . . .
   that I may receive
      the gift I need,
         so I may become
            the gifts others need.

Let the Star of Morning Rise

Lord God,
in the deepest night
there rises the star of morning,
    of birth,
        the herald of a new day you are making,
a day of great joy dawning
    in yet faint shafts
        of light and love.

I hear whispers of peace in the stillness,
fresh breezes of promise
    stirring,
winter sparrows
    chirping of life,
a baby's cry
    of need
        and hope —
            Christmas!

In the darkness I see the light
    and find in it comfort,
        confidence,
            cause for celebration,
for the darkness cannot overcome it;
and I rejoice to nourish it
    in myself,
        in other people,
            in the world
for the sake of him
    in whom it was born
        and shines forever,
            even Jesus the Christ.

Other LuraMedia Publications

BANKSON, MARJORY ZOET
Braided Streams:
Esther and a Woman's Way of Growing
Seasons of Friendship:
Naomi and Ruth as a Pattern
"This Is My Body. . .":
Creativity, Clay, and Change

BOHLER, CAROLYN STAHL
Prayer on Wings: *A Search for Authentic Prayer*

DOHERTY, DOROTHY ALBRACHT
and McNAMARA, MARY COLGAN
Out of the Skin Into the Soul:
The Art of Aging

GEIGER, LURA JANE
and PATRICIA BACKMAN
Braided Streams Leader's Guide
and SUSAN TOBIAS
Seasons of Friendship Leader's Guide

GOODSON, WILLIAMSON (with Dale J.)
Re-Souled: *Parallel Spiritual Awakening of a
Psychiatrist and His Patient in Alcohol Recovery*

JEVNE, RONNA FAY
It All Begins With Hope:
Patients, Caretakers, and the Bereaved Speak Out
and ALEXANDER LEVITAN
No Time for Nonsense:
Getting Well Against the Odds

KEIFFER, ANN
Gift of the Dark Angel: *A Woman's Journey
through Depression toward Wholeness*

LODER, TED
Eavesdropping on the Echoes:
Voices from the Old Testament
Guerrillas of Grace:
Prayers for the Battle
Tracks in the Straw:
Tales Spun from the Manger
Wrestling the Light:
Ache and Awe in the Human-Divine Struggle

MEYER, RICHARD C.
One Anothering:
Biblical Building Blocks for Small Groups

MILLETT, CRAIG
In God's Image:
Archetypes of Women in Scripture

O'CONNOR, ELIZABETH
Search for Silence *(Revised Edition)*

PRICE, H.H.
Blackberry Season:
A Time to Mourn, A Time to Heal

RAFFA, JEAN BENEDICT
The Bridge to Wholeness:
A Feminine Alternative to the Hero Myth

SAURO, JOAN
Whole Earth Meditation:
Ecology for the Spirit

SCHAPER, DONNA
Stripping Down:
The Art of Spiritual Restoration

WEEMS, RENITA J.
Just a Sister Away: *A Womanist Vision
of Women's Relationships in the Bible*
I Asked for Intimacy: *Stories of Blessings,
Betrayals, and Birthings*

The Women's Series

BORTON, JOAN
Drawing from the Women's Well:
Reflections on the Life Passage of Menopause

CARTLEDGE-HAYES, MARY
To Love Delilah:
Claiming the Women of the Bible

DUERK, JUDITH
Circle of Stones:
Woman's Journey to Herself
I Sit Listening to the Wind:
A Woman's Encounter within Herself

**O'HALLORAN, SUSAN and
DELATTRE, SUSAN**
The Woman Who Lost Her Heart:
A Tale of Reawakening

RUPP, JOYCE
The Star in My Heart:
Experiencing Sophia, Inner Wisdom

SCHNEIDER-AKER, KATHERINE
God's Forgotten Daughter:
*A Modern Midrash: What If
Jesus Had Been A Woman?*

LuraMedia, Inc. , 7060 Miramar Rd., Suite 104, San Diego, CA 92121